FATHERS, MOTHERS, SISTERS, BROTHERS

A Collection of Family Poems

Poems by **MARY ANN HOBERMAN**

Illustrations by **MARYLIN HAFNER**

JOY STREET BOOKS

Little, Brown and Company
Boston Toronto London

This book is dedicated with love to its readers.
"We are all one family."

Text copyright © 1991 by Mary Ann Hoberman
Illustrations copyright © 1991 by Marylin Hafner

First Edition

Library of Congress Cataloging-in-Publication Data

Hoberman, Mary Ann.
    Fathers, mothers, sisters, brothers : a collection of family
poems / poems by Mary Ann Hoberman ; illustrations by Marylin
Hafner. — 1st ed.
        p.   cm.
    Summary: Humorous and serious poems celebrate every
kind of family member, including mothers and fathers, aunts
and uncles, stepbrothers, stepsisters, and cousins.
    ISBN 0-316-36736-2
    1. Family — Juvenile poetry.   2. Children's poetry,
American.   [1. Family life — Poetry.   2. American
poetry.]   I. Hafner, Marylin, ill.   II. Title.
    PS3558.03367F38   1991
    811'.54 — dc20   90-43222

Joy Street Books are published by
Little, Brown and Company (Inc.)

10 9 8 7 6 5 4 3 2 1

WOR

Published simultaneously in Canada
by Little, Brown & Company (Canada) Limited

Printed in the United States of America

What is a family?
Who is a family?
One and another makes two is a family!
Baby and father and mother: a family!
Parents and sister and brother: a family!

All kinds of people can make up a family
All kinds of mixtures can make up a family

What is a family?
Who is a family?
The children that lived in a shoe is a family!
A pair like a kanga and roo is a family!
A calf and a cow that go moo is a family!

All kinds of creatures can make up a family
All kinds of numbers can make up a family

What is a family?
Who is a family?
Either a lot or a few is a family;
But whether there's ten or there's two in *your* family,
All of your family plus *you* is a family!

MY BABY BROTHER

My baby brother's beautiful,
So perfect and so tiny.
His skin is soft and velvet brown;
His eyes are dark and shiny.

His hair is black and curled up tight;
His two new teeth are sharp and white.
I like it when he chews his toes;
And when he laughs, his dimple shows.

FOUR GENERATIONS

Sometimes when we go out for walks,
I listen while my father talks.

The thing he talks of most of all
Is how it was when he was small

And he went walking with *his* dad
And conversations that they had

About *his* father and the talks
They had when *they* went out for walks.

BIG SISTER

I have a big sister;
She's taller and older;
On tiptoe I only
Reach up to her shoulder;
But I have a secret
That I haven't told her.
(It's how to grow faster
Until I grow past her.)

I watch what she's eating;
I watch what she's drinking;
I don't let her notice
Or see what I'm thinking;
But each time that she
Takes a bite, I take two;
And that way she only
Eats half what I do.

I have a big sister;
She's taller and older;
On tiptoe I only
Reach up to her shoulder;
But I have a secret
That I haven't told her.
(The way I will beat her
Is just to outeat her!)

PICK UP YOUR ROOM

Pick up your room, my mother says
(She says it every day);
My room's too heavy to pick up
(That's what I always say).

Drink up your milk, she says to me,
Don't bubble like a clown;
Of course she knows I'll answer that
I'd rather drink it down.

And when she says at eight o'clock,
You must go right to bed,
We both repeat my answer:
Why not go left instead?

GRANDMAS AND GRANDPAS

My grandma's face is rosy red;
She wears a scarf around her head;
And when she tucks me into bed,
She plants three kisses on my head.

And in the spring she always makes
A garden which she hoes and rakes;
She rubs my tummy when it aches
And bakes me special birthday cakes.

My other grandma's face is pale;
She sends me letters in the mail;
She taught me how to play the scale,
And once she wrote a fairy tale.

She knits me mittens, scarves, and socks;
She helps build castles with my blocks;
And when I got the chicken pox,
She let me have her button box.

My grandpa's fat but not too fat;
He likes to wear a cowboy hat;
He tells my grandma's cat to scat
(My grandma doesn't much like that).

He tells me stories that are true
Of all the things he used to do;
Sometimes he takes me to the zoo;
He's teaching me to yodel, too.

My other grandpa's thin and tall,
Which makes him good at basketball.
He visits us each spring and fall
And takes me walking in the mall;

We pick out things we'd like to own,
Like sailboats or a saxophone;
And when we're tired to the bone,
He treats me to an ice-cream cone.

RELATIVES

When relatives come visit us,
They pinch my cheek and make a fuss;
They chuck my chin and call me lamb
And say how nice and big I am.
They pat my head and call me dear
And talk as if I couldn't hear:

"He's got his Uncle Perry's nose
And Cousin Charlie's chubby toes
And Emma's ears and Julian's skin
And Aunt Meg's freckles on his chin.
His voice is just like Grandpa's was;
He blinks the way that Grandma does;
He's got the family's hazel eyes;
He'll likely reach his father's size.
He looks a tiny bit too thin
But that's because of Carolyn.
He has his mother's knobby knees
And Grandma's brother's allergies.
They says he is a little wild
And stubborn, like Naomi's child
(The one who wasn't very smart).
His father says he's good in art
The same as he was years ago;
They both take after Cousin Joe,

And didn't Denny draw and paint?
Remember how she used to faint?
Her father fainted too, they say;
When he was ten, his hair turned gray;
It passed on to his older son
(Or was it to the younger one?)
They were quite handsome even so;
They both resembled Cousin Joe,
The other one, who moved to Greece
And was left-handed like his niece.
His hair is more like Jack's although
He looks a little more like Joe."

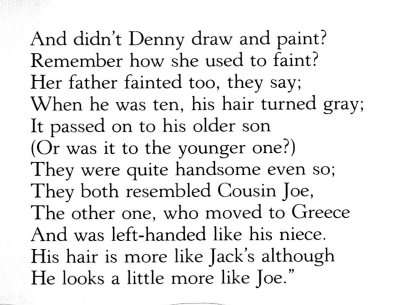

And while I go on standing there
And they keep mussing up my hair
And calling me a little lamb,
I wonder who I *really* am.

NEW JACKET

I've got a new jacket.
I don't even care.
What good is a jacket
You can't even wear?
    A not-everyday jacket
    That's-not-for-play jacket
    Do-as-I-say jacket
Just isn't fair.

It's yellow and red
With a zigzag design.
They bought it for me
And they said it was mine.
    A must-keep-it-neat jacket
    Not-for-the-street jacket
    Don't-you-look-sweet jacket
Isn't that fine?

I think that they bought it
Just so they could say
Go take off that jacket,
Don't wear it today.
    A don't-get-it-messed jacket
    Please-keep-it-pressed jacket
    That-is-your-best jacket
Put it away.

SICK DAYS

On days when I am sick in bed
My mother is so nice;
She brings me bowls of chicken soup
And ginger ale with ice.

She cuts the crusts off buttered toast
And serves it on a tray
And sits down while I eat it
And doesn't go away.

She reads my favorite books to me;
She lets me take my pick;
And everything is perfect —
Except that I am sick!

MY UNCLE

My uncle has a twinkle
    In his eye
    In his eye
And every time he sees me
    He says "Hi"
    He says "Hi"
And every time he leaves me
    He says "Bye"
    He says "Bye"
With a winkle and a blinkle
    And a twinkle
    In his eye.

COUSINS ARE COZY

Cousins are cozy
Wherever they're from;
They feel like your family
Whenever they come.
Some people have many;
Most people have some.
Cousins are cozy
Wherever they're from.

SOMETIMES

Sometimes I like to be alone
And look up at the sky
And think my thoughts inside my head —
Just me, myself, and I.

AN ONLY CHILD

An only child's the only one
And that can be a lot of fun

You don't take turns;
You needn't share
Or drag a baby
Everywhere.

No one's around
To break your toys
Or tease
Or make a lot of noise
Or grab the biggest piece of pie
Or tell on you when it's a lie.

You get the front seat in the car;
No one's more favorite than you are;
On holidays you're special, too,
And all the presents are for you.

An only child's the only one
And that can be a lot of fun

I HAVE
NOTHING
TO DO.

An only child's the one and only
And that can be a little lonely

You needn't share your toys, it's true,
But no one's there to share with you
Or play with on a rainy day
Or when your friends have gone away.

And what is more, there's no one there
When your parents aren't fair
Or when your parents aren't there.

Sometimes you'd like to take a rest,
Have someone else to be the best,
Have someone else to take the blame,
Not always have them call *your* name.

An only child's the one and only
And that can be a little lonely

Now all of this is surely true;
But if there's more than one of you,
Here is a fact you have to face:
Sometimes you must take second place.
But when you're one, it's all reversed:
An only child is *always first!*

MISS MCGILLICUDDY

When our old baby-sitter quit,
Another sitter came to sit.
She told us as she did the split,
    "I am not a fuddy-duddy.
    I am Miss McGillicuddy."

While she touched her toes, she said,
"Homework should be done in bed.
Rest is best to clear your head.
    First you snooze and then you study."
    So said Miss McGillicuddy.

When it rains, she doesn't fret;
That's because she likes to get
Dripping, dropping, sopping wet.
    "I don't mind if I am muddy."
    Silly Miss McGillicuddy!

"EAT IT — IT'S GOOD FOR YOU!"

"Eat it — it's good for you!"
    That makes me mad.
How can something good for you
    Taste so bad?

"Try it. You'll like it."
    I know that's a lie.
I know I won't like it
    So why should I try?

"Just take a nibble.
    Just one little taste."
What good is a nibble?
    The rest goes to waste.

Eggplant is icky.
    Spaghetti is fine.
Why can't they eat their food
    And let me eat mine?

AGATHA, AGATHA

Agatha, Agatha, honestly, Agatha!
Why can't you hurry and put on your clothes?
Why do you dawdle, why *must* you procrastinate,
Knotting your laces and blowing your nose?

Agatha, Agatha, honestly, Agatha!
Please pay attention and tie up that shoe!
Breakfast's been ready for over an hour;
Everyone's sitting there waiting for *you!*

Agatha, Agatha, honestly, Agatha!
Tuck in your blouse, it's all caught in a bunch!
You're such a slowpoke, you dilly and dally;
Don't you know everyone's eating their lunch?

Agatha, Agatha, honestly, Agatha!
It's growing later and you're growing thinner.
If you don't button your sweater this minute,
I have a feeling you might miss your dinner.

Agatha, Agatha, honestly, Agatha!
Now that you're dressed and you want to be fed,
Dinner is over so take off your clothes again,
Put on pajamas and get into bed.

WHEN ANNIE WAS ADOPTED

When Annie was adopted,
Her brand-new brother smiled;
He thought they were so lucky
To have a brand-new child.

He gave her tiny tickles,
Some kisses and a hug;
He tucked her in her basket
And wrapped her nice and snug;

And just before she fell asleep,
She looked at him and smiled
As though she knew already
She was their brand-new child.

HALF-WHOLE-STEP

I *have* a half-sister
I *have* a whole-sister
I *have* a step-sister
　　That adds up to three.

I *am* a half-brother
I *am* a whole-brother
I *am* a step-brother
　　There's just one of me!

MY FATHER

My father doesn't live with us.
It doesn't help to make a fuss;
But still I feel unhappy, plus
    I miss him.

My father doesn't live with me.
He's got another family;
He moved away when I was three.
    I miss him.

I'm always happy on the day
He visits and we talk and play;
But after he has gone away
    I miss him.

THE LITTLE SISTER STORE

When my silly little sister
Knocks my blocks down on the floor,
I tell her I will sell her
At the little sister store.

She knows I'm only joking,
That there isn't such a shop;
But even though she knows it —
At least it makes her stop!

MY BIG BROTHERS

When my big brothers have a fight,
Each one thinks that he is right.
(The only time that they agree
Is when they both gang up on *me!*)

DINNERTIME

David asks for his dessert
Peggy wants to press her skirt
She has dance class and she's late
David says he cannot wait
Mike is giving him a ride
He'll just go and wait outside
Father tells him he will not
David mutters thanks a lot
Ann says she expects a call
Benjamin won't eat at all
Mother starts to serve the pie
Benjamin begins to cry
Mother asks him what is wrong
Father says the tea's too strong
Ann gets up to get the phone
Benjamin begins to moan
Peggy says her tights are torn
David says he hears a horn
Father says to finish first
David says that he will burst
Peggy says it isn't fair

Ann has on her other pair
Now she will be late for class
Benjamin upsets his glass
David's taking tiny bites
Ann is taking off the tights
David says the crust is tough
Mother says she's had enough
Father says it's not too bad
Mother says she's going mad
David wiggles like a mouse
That is dinner at our house.

25

SHY

Sometimes when I don't want to go
To visit someone I don't know,
They never stop to ask me why.
    She's shy
    They say
    She's shy

Or if we're leaving someone's house,
They say I'm quiet as a mouse
When I forget to say good-bye.
    She's shy
    They say
    She's shy

Cat's got her tongue, they always say,
She often does clam up this way,
She's silent as a stone today.
    She's shy
    They say
    She's shy

I am not shy — or if I am
I'm not a mouse or stone or clam.
I like to look and listen to
What other people say and do.
If I can't think of things to say,
Why should I say things anyway?
    I don't see why
    That makes me shy

WHEN I GROW UP

When I grow up, I want to be
A grown-up who remembers me
And what it felt like to be small:
How much I liked to bounce a ball
And pump my swing high in the air
And think of flying everywhere.
How scared I was of doors that creak
Or being it in hide-and-seek
Or if my parents had a fight
Or when I had bad dreams at night.
How much I hated loud machines
And slimy worms and lima beans.
What fun it was to dig a hole,
To make a cake and lick the bowl,
To ride my bike all afternoon,
To plan on going to the moon,
To find an egg inside a nest
And have my best friend like me best.

VACATION

In my head I hear a humming:
Summer summer summer's coming.
Soon we're going on vacation
But there is a complication:
Day by day the problem's growing —
We don't know yet where we're going!

Mother likes the country best;
That's so she can read and rest.
Dad thinks resting is a bore;
He's for fishing at the shore.

WOW!

Sailing is my brother's pick;
Sailing makes my sister sick;
She says swimming's much more cool,
Swimming in a swimming pool.
As for me, why, I don't care,
I'd be happy anywhere!

In my head I hear a humming:
Summer summer summer's coming.
Soon we're going on vacation
But we have a complication:
Day by day the problem's growing —
Where oh where will we be going?

HELLO!

OUR FAMILY COMES FROM 'ROUND THE WORLD

Our family comes
From 'round the world:
Our hair is straight,
Our hair is curled,
Our eyes are brown,
Our eyes are blue,
Our skins are different
Colors, too.

Tra la tra la
Tra la tra lee
We're one big happy family!

We're girls and boys,
We're big and small,
We're young and old,
We're short and tall.
We're everything
That we can be
And still we are
A family.

O la dee da
O la dee dee
We're one big happy family!

We laugh and cry,
We work and play,
We help each other
Every day.
The world's a lovely
Place to be
Because we are
A family.

Hurray hurrah
Hurrah hurree
We're one big happy family!

CONTENTS